101 STORY STARTERS for kids

by

Dena McMurdie

batchofbooks.com

To contact the author about permissions, send an email to
reviewkidsbooks@gmail.com.

ISBN: 9781080810536

Published by Batch of Books.

Interior design and cover design by Dena McMurdie.

Cover art by MisterElements and fearsonline.

First printing, July 2019.

Table of Contents

How to Use This Book:

1. Locate the genre that interests you most.
2. Find a story starter that kicks your imagination into high-gear.
3. Figure out what your characters are doing, how they got into the situation, and how the story will end.
4. Start writing!

Remember, it's your story. You can change the name, gender, or the number of characters in the story. Make the character an animal or an alien. Change the setting. Switch up the point of view. Move the story starter to the middle or end of your story instead of the beginning. Use your imagination and make the story your own!

Questions to ask yourself before you start writing:

1. What are your characters doing? Why are they in this situation?
2. What happens next in the story? You've been given a start, now it's up to you to make it a fantastic story.
3. What are your characters working toward? For example, are they going on a quest, trying to survive, or navigating a friendship? Decide what your character's goal is and build your story around that.
4. How does the story end?

Sofia couldn't believe it. Her new YouTube video had over 500 views. Someone even left a comment. She was going to be famous!

Sofia was going crazy every body was so suprised that she got 500 views

More than anything, Connor wanted to try out for the school play. But there was one giant problem standing in his way. He was terrified of being on stage.

One Day A man named James came to the Mall And he was mostly oil so he Died

Peyton and I have been best friends since kindergarten. Sure, she's spending more time with Kylie lately, but she'll come back to me. Best friends forever, right?

Gavin rushed out of school as soon as he heard the final bell. He looked over his shoulder to make sure nobody was following him, then ducked down the alleyway. If anyone found out where he was going, he would never hear the end of it.

The number on the price tag was more money than Makayla had. Even if she saved her allowance for months, she wouldn't have enough. She almost gave up right then, but Makayla hadn't come this far to quit now. She would get the money—no matter what.

_____

_____

_____

_____

_____

_____

_____

_____

_____

_____

_____

_____

_____

_____

_____

_____

Grandma was on the front porch when Mom and I drove up. She opened my door and pulled me into a big hug.

"I'm so glad you're here for the summer," she said.

_____

_____

_____

_____

_____

_____

_____

_____

_____

_____

_____

_____

_____

_____

_____

_____

_____

_____

_____

_____

Balvan pushed his way over to me and gave me a hard shove.

"I hope you're ready for the game tonight," he sneered. "Because you're going down."

Memo to self: never make a bet you aren't 100% positive you can win. Unfortunately, I wasn't thinking clearly when I bet Jin Lee that my team would beat his in the finals.

Bailey couldn't believe she had to go all the way across the country for the summer. She had to leave all her friends behind. Sure, they could video chat, but it wasn't the same. She was going to miss out on everything fun.

"This place is amazing," said Annie. "It could be our secret hideout!" She looked eagerly around at her friends, watching as their eyes lit up with excitement.

_____

_____

_____

_____

_____

_____

_____

_____

_____

_____

_____

_____

_____

_____

_____

_____

_____

_____

_____

_____

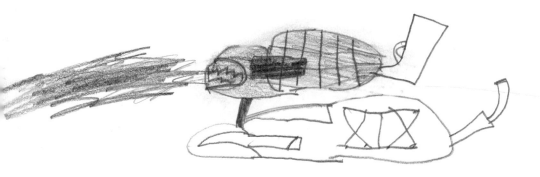

Never in a million years would I have guessed that the waistband on a pair of underpants could stretch this far. But I'm sure glad it can.

Squish.

Gabriel didn't look down to see what he'd stepped in. Based on the smell, he could tell exactly what it was.

"Oops" is a word you never want to hear your best friend say when she's holding a pair of hair clippers and staring at the back of your head.

If James hadn't seen his mashed potatoes move with his own two eyes, he never would have believed it. But there they were, doing a hula dance on his dinner plate.

_____

_____

_____

_____

_____

_____

_____

_____

_____

_____

_____

_____

_____

_____

_____

_____

_____

_____

Ellie watched helplessly as the bull charged toward her. She was really starting to question her choices over the past two weeks. But it wasn't her fault she was in this predicament, not really. Not unless you counted the incident with the chicken. Which she didn't.

Ethan had a knack for getting into trouble. He also had a trick for getting out of it. It all came down to creating a diversion. He pointed in the opposite direction of where he needed to go and yelled, "Free tacos!"

It worked like a charm.

My backpack can hold precisely twelve rolls of duct tape. This may seem like a lot, but sticky situations call for even stickier solutions. Which is why I'm heading to the treehouse with a backpack full of the stickiest duct tape I could find.

Getting handcuffed to the principal's desk was NOT in the plan. Kimiko had specifically drawn a giant red X over the principal's office on the map so they could avoid this exact situation. Now here she was, handcuffed, bored, and wondering where on earth Stella could be.

My mom always says I shouldn't do everything my friends tell me to. I always thought she was just being dramatic. Until now.

_____

_____

_____

_____

_____

_____

_____

_____

_____

_____

_____

_____

_____

_____

_____

_____

_____

_____

_____

Olivia filled both cups of her older sister's bra with the slugs she'd collected earlier. Using the bra like a double-barrelled slingshot, she took aim and fired. The screams that followed were worth the punishment she would receive later.

That reminded her—she needed to return the bra before her sister noticed it was missing.

Deepak never expected to find his favorite teacher laughing hysterically at a squashed fish in the middle of the street. Ms. Mackerel was missing a shoe and had a fishing net perched on her head like a bizarre hat.

Anyone who claims that frogs turn into princes when you kiss them has obviously never tried it. I've kissed every frog in southern Louisiana and not one of those slimy critters looked any different afterward.

Until today.

Nicolas glared into the beady little eyes, refusing to blink, refusing to look away. The skunk stared right back. There was no telling how long this epic battle of wills would last.

Slowly, the skunk lifted her bushy black and white striped tail. Nicolas could have sworn he saw the skunk smile right before she unleashed her spray into the air.

Raiden always joked that he could turn anything into a grease spot by sitting on it. Now, looking between the empty hamster cage and the unidentifiable smear on the seat of his chair, he was truly afraid he might be right.

Everyone said it was impossible. Don't even try. Which is exactly why I had to do it. Nobody becomes famous without taking a few risks.

I pulled the goggles over my eyes and got into position.

Historical Fiction

The advertisement said Old Tom was looking to hire ranch hands for the summer. Must be able to ride, shoot, and rope a calf.

Papa always said I was a born rider, just like his Pa before him. And now that I'm old enough, I can learn the other things too.

We're headed to the march. Mama says it's important, that it could change things. Last night, she helped Sis and me paint big red letters onto cardboard signs and fix them to sticks for holding.

Everyone says the roan stallion Mr. Sanders captured is unrideable. He threw six grown men already. But I've always had a special way with horses. If I could just spend some time with him, I'd have that roan as tame as a kitten.

_____

_____

_____

_____

_____

_____

_____

_____

_____

_____

_____

_____

_____

_____

_____

_____

_____

_____

I'm not saying Mr. Tanner is a spy, but I'm not saying he's not. All I'm saying is it's mighty suspicious for an American school teacher to know so much about Russia.

Mary Albright was ready to meet her new governess. She couldn't say the same for her brother, but at least one of them was clean and presentable. Even though she knew it was unlikely, Mary hoped the new governess would have a better sense of humor than the previous four.

Roy pushed open the double doors of the saloon and strolled inside. Big Red sat in the corner, eating. Roy stalked over to Big Red, drew both pistols, and said, "Stick em up, Red."

_____

_____

_____

_____

_____

_____

_____

_____

_____

_____

_____

_____

_____

_____

_____

_____

_____

_____

_____

Pa says there's gold to be had in California. He met a man last night who told him about gold nuggets the size of a man's fist, just lying there for the taking. First thing this morning, Pa started packing our bags.

Mama and Papa wanted a new life. A fresh start. The chance to be part of something big. That's what they told Jacob when they announced they'd bought a parcel of land out west. When spring comes, they said, the whole family was going out there to help start a civilization.

Carrie looked out the train window and watched the countryside flash by. There were too many orphans in the city, the government decided. So she was being sent to another state, somewhere with fewer orphans and more families that needed an extra girl to help out.

Suddenly, I realized that Naveen and I had been transported smack dab into the middle of the civil war. The good news is that I finally knew when we were. The bad news is that I figured it out just as two groups of angry men emerged from the bushes on either side of us and yelled, "attack!"

Charlotte's trunks sat by the door, filled with everything she held dear. Soon, Baxter would be up to fetch them. Charlotte wanted to tear open the trunks, throw her belongings on the floor, and refuse to go. But what good would it do? Father had determined she would go, so she must.

The tall man pressed a note into Charles's palm. "Get this to General Washington," he whispered. "He'll know what it's about."

Charles nodded once, then melted into the night.

If Mother knew that being an apprentice to Master da Vinci really meant being a guinea pig for his inventions, she would insist I leave his employ immediately. Which is exactly why I will never tell her.

William Shakespeare handed David a stack of papers.

"Can you read?" he asked.

"Yes," David stammered, surprised.

"Good. Have these memorized by sundown. You're going onstage tonight."

_____

_____

_____

_____

_____

_____

_____

_____

_____

_____

_____

_____

_____

_____

_____

_____

_____

_____

MYSTERY

Why would a pair of super-sized underwear be lying in the center of the principal's office? Something weird was going on, and I was determined to find out what it was.

_____

_____

_____

_____

_____

_____

_____

_____

_____

_____

_____

_____

_____

_____

_____

_____

_____

_____

With a list of suspects ten miles long, it was unlikely Emma would figure out who was behind the vandalism on her locker. She tried narrowing down her list of suspects by removing her friends, but that only excluded Mr. Sanders, the janitor.

Janson squinted at the chocolate cake sitting primly on his front porch. There was no note and nothing to indicate who left it. Who had given him the cake? And why did they want to keep their identity a secret?

_____

_____

_____

_____

_____

_____

_____

_____

_____

_____

_____

_____

_____

_____

_____

_____

_____

_____

_____

With dogs disappearing left and right, Gabby knew she had to figure out what was going on. Who was taking the dogs, and why did they want them? Most importantly, where were the dogs now?

Mrs. Harper stormed up to Cammie and shook a muddy bra in her face. "Someone has been ruining my laundry again," she seethed.

Uh oh. Cammie needed to figure out who or what was destroying Mrs. Harper's laundry. And fast.

Maggie stared at the broken glass scattered all over the floor. Who would throw a rock through the window of her favorite pizza place? Maggie knew something suspicious was going on, and she was going to find out who was behind it.

Art supplies had quietly disappeared from Ms. Johnson's classroom all year. The only things left were a few oil pastels and some faded construction paper.

Enough was enough, Kayo decided. It was time to figure out who was behind the thefts.

_____

_____

_____

_____

_____

_____

_____

_____

_____

_____

_____

_____

_____

_____

_____

_____

_____

There are many things that could easily go missing from a middle school, but a tuba is not one of them. How could anyone walk out of the school with it and nobody noticed? Diego was determined to find the missing tuba and put it back where it belonged.

_____

_____

_____

_____

_____

_____

_____

_____

_____

_____

_____

_____

_____

_____

_____

_____

_____

_____

An entire cart full of iPads, gone. Someone literally stole from children. Ty knew the school had hosted a "meet the teacher" event on the night the iPads went missing, which meant that almost anyone could have taken them. But who would steal iPads from their own kid's school? It didn't make sense.

Someone or something set fire to Mrs. Barnes shed. Ishaan needed to figure out exactly what happened so he didn't get blamed for it. Again. But who would want to burn down an old lady's shed? And why?

_____

_____

_____

_____

_____

_____

_____

_____

_____

_____

_____

_____

_____

_____

_____

_____

_____

_____

_____

There was no name on the card attached to the flowers in Camila's locker, just a big XOXO at the bottom. Did she have a secret admirer? Who would go through all the trouble of buying flowers, writing a cryptic note, and cracking the combination on her locker, only to keep their identity a secret?

Ronin couldn't stop thinking about the cryptic photo he'd received by text earlier that day. The phone number was restricted and the sender didn't give any clues about their identity. But Ronin loved solving puzzles, and this mysterious text was right up his alley.

Riley and Ling stopped digging and looked down at the giant hole they'd made in the sand. Something lay at the bottom of the hole. How long had it been there? Days? Years? And why was it buried on a busy beach filled with people?

_____

_____

_____

_____

_____

_____

_____

_____

_____

_____

_____

_____

_____

_____

_____

_____

_____

_____

Zoe kicked at a piece of trash. Her beloved forest was filled with garbage. But why would someone dump their trash in the middle of the woods instead of taking it to the dump?

_____

_____

_____

_____

_____

_____

_____

_____

_____

_____

_____

_____

_____

_____

_____

_____

_____

FANTASY

Three magic potions. One choice.

Everything depended on this decision. I reached out, grabbed a vial, and gulped it down all at once. There was no going back.

Magic was illegal, everyone knew that. What they didn't know was that Maggie possessed more magic in her little finger than the rest of the kingdom put together.

Jamal knew the instant the dragon caught his scent. He saw the animal start to circle in the air above his head. His heart leapt into his throat as the dragon tucked its wings and dove toward him.

Carlos had never performed magic before, but it was too late to worry about that now. He would have to learn on the go—starting with the demon rushing toward him. He felt the power building in his wand as he raised it above his head, ready to strike.

Krisha gasped as she pushed aside the last of the branches. Before her lay a lush, green valley, untouched by the modern world. In the distance loomed a single tower made of stone. Krisha stumbled out of the forest and started limping in the direction of the tower.

_____

_____

_____

_____

_____

_____

_____

_____

_____

_____

_____

_____

_____

_____

_____

_____

_____

_____

Fairy godmothers are supposed to swoop in at the last moment and save the day. In reality, all they do is mess things up. If I ever see my fairy godmother again, I plan on running as far and as fast as I can.

_____

_____

_____

_____

_____

_____

_____

_____

_____

_____

_____

_____

_____

_____

_____

_____

_____

_____

_____

Everyone warns you about leprechauns, but nobody says to watch out for fairies. Who knew those cute little ladies could be so dangerous? If I ever find a way out of this, I'll never talk to a fairy again.

_____

_____

_____

_____

_____

_____

_____

_____

_____

_____

_____

_____

_____

_____

_____

_____

_____

_____

Oliver picked up a large, crumbling book and let it fall open in his hands. He blew the dust off the page and squinted to get a better look.

"Woah," he whispered. He was holding an honest to goodness spell-book.

A dash of charisma, a sprinkle of laughter, and a heaping cupful of chocolate chips. Stir no more than 7 turns of the spoon, then bake for 15 minutes.

Easy peasy. Once Jasmine gets a taste of my love muffin, she won't be able to resist my Dad. Who knew that finding a new mom was as easy as following a recipe?

The old wizard placed his staff in my hand.

"It's up to you, now," he whispered. "I've taught you everything you need to know."

The old woman cracked open the door, eyeing us up and down.

I stepped forward. "Sorry to bother you, but we need to call our parents. Can we borrow your phone?"

The woman's eyes crinkled as she smiled wide, her rotten teeth barely hanging on to black gums. She opened the door further. "Of course, children. Come in and I'll see about that phony thing you mentioned."

The prophecy was not what Jayden expected at all, which shouldn't have been surprising—prophecies rarely were. But what was he supposed to do with a cryptic poem that sounded like gibberish?

_____

_____

_____

_____

_____

_____

_____

_____

_____

_____

_____

_____

_____

_____

_____

_____

_____

_____

_____

Lily had always wanted to see a real unicorn in the wild. And now here she was, face to face with one of the magnificent creatures.

Lucas flipped on the kitchen light. "Gotcha!" he yelled, then froze as he gaped at what he saw. The kitchen was full of tiny people, no taller than a pencil, all frozen in place and staring back at him.

"What are you guys?" he stammered.

This was it. The spell that Chloe needed to set everything right. She grabbed the spell off the shelf, tore off the top, and swallowed it down in one gulp.

Max needed to get away, and fast. So he did something he'd never done before. He picked up his time traveling watch. Without looking at it, he spun the dial. He didn't care when or where he ended up. Anytime would be better than right now, right here.

_____

_____

_____

_____

_____

_____

_____

_____

_____

_____

_____

_____

_____

_____

_____

_____

_____

It was finally happening. Ethan's stomach churned as he climbed aboard the spaceship and strapped himself into his seat. He was leaving Earth and he had no idea when he'd be back, if ever.

Kiara didn't know what the world would look like when she woke from cryo-sleep, or even if Earth would exist at all. Choking back her tears, she took one last look out the window before she climbed into her cryopod and waited for sleep to take her.

Greg had heard rumors about video games that were so realistic you felt like you were inside them. He had wanted to play one, to see what it was like. But now that he was inside the game itself, he realized he had no idea how to get out.

Alex stepped inside the old phone booth and picked up the phone's receiver. He didn't lift it to his ear. He didn't need to. As soon as the receiver left the cradle, the booth filled with an otherworldly light. Alex lifted his arms above his head, welcoming the weightless sensation that enveloped him as he levitated up toward the source of the light.

A group of six adults in hazmat suits filed into the room and surrounded me. One of them came forward and took my arm.

"Come with us," she said. "This is more serious than we thought."

A blinding flash of light seared across the night sky, followed a moment later by a bone-jarring boom. Nadia looked worriedly at Chase before both kids started running toward the sound.

Everyone thought humans would have colonized Mars by now. But the future is much different than people expected. Remember all those movies about robots taking over the world? They weren't so far-fetched after all.

Flying a spaceship should be simple, easy. But when all the auto-systems are down and one engine is blown, it's much more difficult. Luckily, I know exactly what I'm doing.

The little orange creatures surrounded me, but I wasn't afraid. They were too cute to be dangerous. Besides, they seemed to like me. Hopefully, they could overlook the fact that I'd appeared out of thin air, covered in steaming trash and smelling like the back end of a mule.

Madeline moaned and opened her eyes. She was in a quiet, white room. Surgical instruments sat on a cart near the wall. A whirring sound made her look down at her arm.

"Oh, no," she whispered.

Brenner wasn't sure what he expected to find behind the locked door. An army of robots, perhaps, but not this. Anything but this.

The GPS tracker indicated a spot in the desert, far from civilization.

"What could be out there?" Avery asked.

"There's only one way to find out," said Miles, handing her a hover-board.

I stared at the little red pill in my hand. This pill had the power to change my life completely. Just one dose would make me bigger, stronger, and smarter than all the other kids my age. It was something I'd never dared to dream about.

HORROR

He smelled it before he saw it. The stench assaulted Alejandro's senses like the ocean invading a beach at high tide. A second later, he heard a growl that sent chills racing down his spine.

There's a legend about the old Bantham house. They say the ghost of Mrs. Bantham still roams the attic and you can hear her crying on every full moon. Of course, my parents say it's just a rumor, that there are no ghosts in our new house. But I'm not so sure.

If you're quiet enough on a still summer night, you can sneak up to the old Winaker shed and peek through the cracks in the boards. The last kid that did it spent two weeks in bed, shivering and sobbing until his parents sent him to live with his great-aunt in another town.

Tonight, it's my turn. I crack my knuckles and steal toward the crumbling structure.

Meet me in the graveyard at sundown.

What's in the graveyard?

You'll see.

I knew I shouldn't go. I also knew that nothing could keep me away.

"Welcome," the creature hissed from deep inside its black hood. "We've been expecting you." The creature extended a clawed hand and pulled back the moth-eaten curtains. "Come in."

I didn't believe in monsters until my English teacher transformed into one right in front of my eyes. She was reading an assignment to the class when she stopped mid-sentence, threw her head back, and let out a howl that stopped my heart. She dropped to all fours as her teeth elongated into fangs and dark hair sprouted from every inch of her body.

The forest loomed dark and foreboding in front of the three kids. The trees seemed to whisper among themselves in a creaking, groaning language. After a quick glance at each other, the kids slipped into the forest, the darkness swallowing them up.

_____

_____

_____

_____

_____

_____

_____

_____

_____

_____

_____

_____

_____

_____

_____

_____

_____

_____

_____

Nobody went swimming in the lake after midnight. Only creatures of the night were brave enough to enter the waters after dark. And Yuan wanted nothing more than to become a creature of the night.

Ebony's heart skipped a beat as she looked out over the water. The gentle rocking of the boat did nothing to dispel the chill that now gripped her. A pale specter hovered in the distance, long robes shifting in the breeze as it moved toward the boat.

Tyrone stared into a thousand reflections of himself. No matter which way he turned, there was another mirror, each one reflecting off all the others. How would he find his way out of here?

Just then, Tyrone saw a dark shadow flit across the infinite reflections.

_____

_____

_____

_____

_____

_____

_____

_____

_____

_____

_____

_____

_____

_____

_____

_____

_____

_____

_____

_____

Amara couldn't sleep. The old house creaked and moaned as it settled in for the night. Footsteps sounded on the floor above. Who would be skittering around the attic in the middle of the night? Amara slipped out of bed and made her way up the creaky stairs that led to the attic.

Wallace and Ginny huddled as close to the fire as they dared, watching the shadows dance beyond the circle of light. Nightmares lurked in the dark, green eyes glowing as they waited. Then, with no warning, the fire went out.

_____

_____

_____

_____

_____

_____

_____

_____

_____

_____

_____

_____

_____

_____

_____

_____

_____

_____

_____

Kate found the grave with no trouble. It was fresh, the dirt unsettled from the funeral earlier that day. When she struck the ground with her shovel, it got stuck. Kate flicked on her flashlight to see what her shovel was caught on. A human hand was wrapped around the bottom of the handle, holding it tight. Kate gasped and stumbled backward as a second hand burst out of the grave.

114

Simon barely had time to register the sensation of something slippery winding around his ankle before it pulled him under the water.

The woman's grin widened, showing off two rows of pointed teeth and a forked tongue. Startled, Rowan took a step toward the door, but the woman moved faster than he thought possible. She lunged forward and caught his wrist in her cold, scaly hand.

"Going somewhere?" she hissed.

About Batch of Books

Batch of Books is a blog dedicated to finding great books for children and teens. It features reading lists, giveaways, freebies, quizzes, and other fun content.

Visit us online at www.batchofbooks.com.

If you enjoyed this book, please consider leaving a review.

Write and draw your own comics, cartoons, and graphic novels with these blank comic books!

Visit

BATCH OF BOOKS

batchofbooks.com

Picture Credits:

Made in the USA
Lexington, KY
20 November 2019